*Other PaperStars by Jean Fritz*

AROUND THE WORLD IN A HUNDRED YEARS
BULLY FOR YOU, TEDDY ROOSEVELT!
MAKE WAY FOR SAM HOUSTON
STONEWALL
THE GREAT LITTLE MADISON
TRAITOR: The Case of Benedict Arnold
HARRIET BEECHER STOWE AND
  THE BEECHER PREACHERS

*Elizabeth Cady Stanton*

# You Want Women to Vote, Lizzie Stanton?

## JEAN FRITZ

*illustrated by* DyAnne DiSalvo-Ryan

Penguin Putnam Books for Young Readers

Text copyright © 1995 by Jean Fritz.

Illustrations copyright © 1995 by DyAnne DiSalvo-Ryan.

A PaperStar Book, published in 1999 by Penguin Putnam Books for Young Readers,
345 Hudson Street, New York, NY 10014.

PaperStar is a registered trademark of The Putnam Berkley Group, Inc.

The PaperStar logo is a trademark of The Putnam Berkley Group, Inc.

Originally published in 1995 by G. P. Putnam's Sons.

Published simultaneously in Canada. Printed in the United States of America.

Book designed by Patrick Collins. Text set in Bembo.

Library of Congress Cataloging-in-Publication Data

Fritz, Jean. You want women to vote, Lizzie Stanton? / Jean Fritz; illustrated by DyAnne
DiSalvo-Ryan. p. cm. Includes bibliographical references and index.
1. Stanton, Elizabeth Cady, 1815-1902—Juvenile literature. 2. Feminists—United
States—Biography—Juvenile literature. 3. Suffragists—United States—Biography—
Juvenile literature. 4. Women—Suffrage—United States—History—Juvenile literature.
[1. Stanton, Elizabeth Cady, 1815-1902. 2. Feminists. 3. Women's rights—History.
4. Women—Suffrage—History. 5. Women—Biography.] I. Disalvo-Ryan, Dyanne, ill.
II. Title.   HQ1413.S67F75  1995   324.6′23′092—dc20   [B]  94-30018  CIP  AC
ISBN 0-698-11764-6

40th Printing

*To Tina*

# You Want Women to Vote, Lizzie Stanton?

# CHAPTER ONE

Yes, Elizabeth Cady Stanton did want women to vote. It was an outlandish idea, but that's what she wanted. Not at first. As a child, she knew that girls didn't count for much, but she didn't expect to change that.

First she had to grow up. She was born Elizabeth Cady in 1815 in Johnstown, New York—a gloomy-looking town that cowered beneath poplar trees. Elizabeth hated poplar trees. They stalked down the main street, unbending, stiff with pride. In the spring they let loose thousands of dangling yellow inchworms, which dropped, like an obscene kind of weather, on people passing beneath. If you had been around then, you might have seen three little girls, their hands over their heads, dodging the trees, racing for home.

They were the Cady sisters—Elizabeth (or Lizzie), Harriet (five years older than Elizabeth), and Margaret (three years younger). You couldn't miss them. They were dressed alike, always in red dresses, black aprons, red stockings, red mittens, red coats, and red hoods. Elizabeth hated red. And she hated the prickly, starched ruffles around the necks of the dresses. Sometimes she might run a finger between her neck and the ruffle, but that wasn't ladylike, her mother said. Grown men could tear off their collars and ties and throw them down, but she was a girl and she couldn't even fool with a ruffle. Elizabeth must learn to crochet, knit, and embroider. To anything that Elizabeth wanted to do, her mother would say no. Anything Elizabeth disliked was exactly what her mother wanted. And who could stand up to Mrs. Cady? Almost six feet tall, she towered over the girls like a poplar tree, dropping her no's, her "everlasting no! no! no!" as if that was the only word that she trusted.

Elizabeth carried some of her childhood likes and dislikes right through her life. Never as a grown woman, for instance, would she wear red. As for embroidering, she thought it was pitiful the way some women used up their energy embroidering "cats on the toe of some slipper, or tulips on an apron." It was enough to make "angels weep," she said.

What Elizabeth did like to do was to visit her father, Judge Cady, in his law office. Sometimes she was allowed to sit in a corner of the room and listen to his clients as they poured out their problems. Often she got angry, particularly if the clients were women. Her father seldom seemed able to help women. Flora Campbell, for instance, had bought her family's farm with her own money, but when her husband died, he had willed it to their son. And he didn't take care of it. What was more, he was mean to her. What could she do?

Nothing, Judge Cady replied. When she married, she became, in the eyes of the law, an "extension" of her husband.

2

All that she owned, all that she earned, even her children became her husband's property to do with as he chose. And he chose to give the farm to a good-for-nothing son.

As soon as Flora Campbell left, Elizabeth exploded. How could the law be so unfair? she asked. Judge Cady took down from his shelves a big law book and showed Elizabeth the law in print.

There was only one thing to do, Elizabeth decided. She would cut that law right out of her father's book. No, her father said. That would do no good. Not even if she cut the law out of all the copies of the book in New York State. The law was made by legislators—all men—in the state capital at Albany, and only they could change it.

Elizabeth had never heard of anything so ridiculous. No wonder men thought they were special. No wonder fathers preferred sons to daughters. And here were the Cadys with five daughters: Tryphena (the oldest) and Catherine (the youngest), in addition to Harriet, Elizabeth, and Margaret. The family couldn't seem to hang on to boys. Three sons (two Daniels and one James) had been born and died before Elizabeth came along, and now only Eleazar was left. Nine years older than Elizabeth, he was both smart and brave as a boy was supposed to be. And of course he was the apple of his father's eye.

But when Elizabeth was eleven years old, Eleazar died. He had just graduated from Union College, and before anyone realized what was happening, the church bells were tolling for him. Elizabeth hated the sound of those church bells. "No, no, no," they seemed to say. No without end. Still, it was her father who broke her heart. Sitting beside the coffin, Judge

5

Cady looked so haggard, so forlorn, so empty that Elizabeth slipped onto his lap to comfort him.

Judge Cady sighed. "I wish you were a boy!" he said.

Of course Elizabeth could never be a boy. Still, perhaps she could make it up to her father if she became just as good as a boy, as smart and brave as Eleazar had been. So that's what she'd do. To be smart, she would study Greek. To be brave, she would learn to ride a horse so well that she would be able to jump fences—even high fences.

The first chance she had, she persuaded the preacher next door to give her Greek lessons. And she took out the fastest horse in her father's stable for a ride. She knew it would take time to become smart and brave, but in the end her father would surely say what she wanted to hear. "Elizabeth," he would say, "you are just as good as any boy."

Before long Mrs. Cady did have one more baby. It was a boy, but he didn't last either. The church bells tolled again, but this time when the family walked to the graveyard, Edward Bayard walked with them. He was studying law with Judge Cady and would soon marry Tryphena.

Elizabeth liked him. He taught her to jump her horse across ditches and over fences. Gradually the fences became higher. Two feet, three feet, and when she began clearing four-foot fences, her father must have heard about it. But he didn't say what she wanted to hear. Nor did he say anything when Elizabeth's Greek teacher bragged about how well she was doing. Nor when Elizabeth was put into the highest class of mathematics and languages at Johnstown Academy. She was the only girl in the class and did every bit as well as the boys, but still—not a word. Then when she was sixteen and finishing at the Academy, she won a prize in Greek. *Now,* she thought. Now he would say it. She rushed home with the Bible she'd won, and put it on her father's desk.

Judge Cady picked it up and sighed. "If only you'd been a boy," he said.

Of course Elizabeth was disappointed, but she was not a person who brooded. Now that she had graduated from the Academy, she knew exactly what she wanted to do next. She wanted to go to Union College, where the boys in her class were going.

But Union College did not accept girls, she was told. There was no college in the country where boys and girls could go together. Elizabeth had never heard of anything so ridiculous. People were always dividing up the world between men and women. "Men here," they said—going where they pleased, making money, doing business, governing, voting. "Women there," they said—staying home, tending the children, obeying the men, being ladylike. Women had to be careful not to step into the men's world. Indeed, they must not even speak out in public before a mixed audience. Obviously Judge Cady went along with this men-women business, and now that Elizabeth was sixteen, he expected her to go along with it too. He told Elizabeth that she would be going to Emma Willard's Female Seminary in Troy. A school just for girls. All learning to be ladies, Elizabeth supposed.

As it turned out, there was far more learning at Emma Willard than training to be ladies, but still Elizabeth was glad when the two years at the seminary were over.

What next?

# CHAPTER TWO

For the most part Elizabeth did what her friends were doing. She went to parties and she visited. Her favorite place to visit was the home of her cousin Libby Smith in Peterboro, New York. Libby's father, Gerrit Smith, was a reformer dedicated to the cause of abolition—or freeing the slaves. His house was a station on the Underground Railroad for slaves making their way to freedom in the North. And it was a meeting place for other abolitionists. People at the Smith house didn't talk about obeying laws; they talked about justice. Even the women talked. Elizabeth had never been with such brilliant minds. She had never felt her own mind climb so high. But when she went home, she didn't talk about the conversations at Peterboro. Judge Cady was against the abolition movement and wouldn't even let it be mentioned in his house. Moreover, he disapproved of Gerrit Smith.

At home Elizabeth joined a group of her friends at church who were helping a poor young man to become a minister.

They raised money to send him through theological school, and when he graduated, they bought him a new broadcloth suit, a high hat, and a cane, and invited him to preach his first sermon in their church. Dressed in their finest clothes, Elizabeth and her friends filed into the church, settled down in the front pew, and looked up at the pulpit. But as soon as the new preacher began to talk, they knew they had wasted their money. His text was, "I suffer not a woman to speak in church." He was preaching about the inferiority of women.

Elizabeth Cady rose to her feet, marched down the aisle and out the church door. Her friends followed.

Elizabeth continued going to Peterboro throughout the 1830s. Her favorite picture of herself at this period shows a small, vivacious young woman with curly brown hair. Some might have said she was pretty, but Elizabeth liked the picture because she thought she looked "so self-asserting and defiant." In any case, she appealed to Henry Stanton, who joined the Smiths' guests in the fall of 1839. Henry was a fiery abolitionist who hoped to go into politics one day. Although Elizabeth, who was now twenty-four years old, was interested in what Henry had to say, it was the man himself who took her breath away. Ten years older than Elizabeth, Henry was tall, handsome, and dramatic-looking.

He had only one drawback. He was engaged to be married. Or so it was said. When he invited Elizabeth to join him for a horseback ride one day, she supposed he simply wanted a companion. But, as it turned out, Henry was not engaged. The two of them were deep in the woods when suddenly Henry asked her to marry him. Elizabeth was completely taken by surprise. Still, she was not too surprised to give an immediate answer. "Yes," she said. Just like that. Then the two went back to the Smiths' house to announce their news.

Like everyone in the household, Gerrit Smith was pleased, but he warned Elizabeth that her father wouldn't like it.

And Judge Cady didn't. Henry Stanton was unsuitable in every way, he said. Not only was he an abolitionist, he was too old for her. And how did he expect to support her? He wouldn't make much money lecturing and, as far as Judge Cady could figure out, Henry's family did not have the means to help him. Did he expect to live off the Cady money?

Elizabeth stood toe-to-toe with her father. Henry was a self-made man, she pointed out. He'd managed before, and he would now. Of course he was older, but if she didn't care, why should her father? As for being an abolitionist, so were many good people. Elizabeth's father would not let up, and soon he was joined by Edward Bayard, who had always been Elizabeth's friend and taken her side. Day after day they argued until Elizabeth felt worn down. Have I made a mistake? she asked herself. Maybe she had been too hasty, so she wrote to Henry, breaking off the engagement. Yet they continued to write to each other, so it didn't seem like a never-again, end-of-the-world good-bye. Indeed, Henry said he considered this only a postponement. And one day in the spring he wrote her that he had been elected a delegate to the World Anti-Slavery Convention in London. If they were married now, they could go to London together. Otherwise, he would be gone for eight months.

This was too much for Elizabeth. If they hurried, not only would she have Henry, she would see London too! They'd just have to elope. And on May 1, 1840, they did. Elizabeth couldn't have a fancy wedding, but she did have something to say about the wording of the ceremony. She and Henry would be equal partners, she explained to the minister, so she would not promise to "obey" him. The service lasted only a few minutes, but when it was over, there was Elizabeth Cady turned into Mrs. Stanton. But never Mrs. Henry Stanton. Henry was not her name and she shouldn't be addressed as if she were just an "extension" of her husband. Since she didn't want to give up her own name, she signed herself Elizabeth Cady Stanton. Throughout her life, some people used her full name; some just said Mrs. Stanton; some called her Cady; and many used her nickname, Lizzie. Henry had his own name for her—Lizzie Lee.

On June 12 Henry and Elizabeth set sail for London. Her sister Harriet and her husband, Daniel Eaton, came to see them off. When it was time to say good-bye, Daniel started a game of tag with Elizabeth. He chased her all over the ship, and of course Elizabeth attracted attention, particularly that of Mr. Birney, a fellow passenger and fellow delegate to the convention. All across the Atlantic, Mr. Birney worried that Elizabeth, with her high spirits, would be an embarrassment to the American delegation. What would the English think of her? In the company of strangers, for instance, she addressed her husband as if they were in their own bedroom. "Henry," she called him, instead of "Mr. Stanton," the way married folk were expected to talk. In spite of Mr. Birney's criticism, however, Elizabeth didn't seem to improve.

One day looking at the ship's mast, she suddenly wanted to see the view from the top. She moved a chair close to the mast, sat in it, and asked the captain to haul her up to the masthead. Going up, she was free as a bird. But when she came down, there was Mr. Birney, glaring at her.

Mr. Birney had only one redeeming feature. He liked to play chess. So did Elizabeth, and she was good at it. Mr. Birney couldn't say it was bad manners for Elizabeth to beat him, and so she often did. She did love to win.

In London, Elizabeth and Henry (and Mr. Birney) stayed at a boarding house, where there were other American delegates, including a group of women. Elizabeth was immediately drawn to Lucretia Mott, a delegate from Philadelphia. A Quaker twenty-two years older than Elizabeth, she was used to other Quakers treating her as an equal to a man. That was the Quaker way. In America, Lucretia lectured on abolition, most often to audiences of women but also to mixed audiences of men and women. Once she provoked a riot in Philadelphia when she insisted that black people be admitted to her lecture. Elizabeth marveled that such a gentle, ladylike person could stand up so staunchly for what she believed was right.

At the London convention, however, Lucretia Mott did not have the chance to do much standing up. When the Americans arrived in England, they were warned that women would not be seated as regular delegates. Although Elizabeth was not a delegate, she was so angry that she spoke her mind at the boarding house, along with Lucretia Mott and the other American women.

Henry was not pleased about this. He had already mentioned to Elizabeth that he wished that she were more "demure," but whether he liked it or not, Elizabeth joined Lucretia when they went to the convention. At their arrival,

they were officially informed of the ruling. Women would not be seated with the delegates.

Most of the American delegates, both men and women, protested. (Not Mr. Birney.)

It did no good. Women could not participate in the convention.

But some had been elected.

No women.

In the end, women were allowed to enter the building, but they could not talk. They were not even permitted to sit in the main part of the auditorium with the men. They were pushed into a railed-off area that looked like a section in a church reserved for slaves. William Lloyd Garrison, an extreme abolitionist, was so angry that he joined the women in their pen and sat through the sessions in silence.

Before taking her seat, one of the American women told her husband not to be "simmy-sammy." But Henry was "simmy-sammy." Although he made a lukewarm speech in favor of seating the women, when it came to a vote, he voted against it. After all, he had his future political career to think of. Besides, Henry did not think it was practical for women to push for their own rights. This would weaken the antislavery position, he said.

Actually, the clergymen were the most violent in their opposition to the women. What would God think? they asked. The women might offend "the heavenly hosts." Hard as it was, the women held their tongues until they left the convention. Then Elizabeth and Lucretia, walking arm in arm, let loose their feelings.

Lucretia was a "revelation" to Elizabeth of what a woman could be. She put into words all the half-thought-out opinions, all the feelings that Elizabeth had been keeping to herself for years. Indeed, Elizabeth took "possession" of Lucretia while they were in London. One day they started out for the British Museum, but they never got inside. They were so busy talking, they sat down on the steps of the museum and for hours reviewed the wrongs that women suffered. On and on they talked, and when they parted, they agreed that sometime they would work together for woman's rights.

Still, it was eight years before Elizabeth and Lucretia fulfilled this promise. In everyday life woman's rights seemed always to take second place to woman's work.

# CHAPTER THREE

Elizabeth Cady Stanton prided herself on her ability to cope with difficulties. She never became seasick, for instance, as so many did on board ship. Even in the roughest gales, there she'd be, walking the deck, fit as a fiddle. Indeed, the only thing she'd ever dreaded was her father's anger, but on returning from Europe, she found that she and Henry were accepted into the family as if there never had been trouble between them. Judge Cady even agreed to take on Henry as a law student, so for a year Elizabeth and Henry lived with her parents.

Then they moved to Boston, where Henry opened a law practice and Elizabeth became mistress of her own home and mother to a growing family. Between 1842 and 1845 she gave birth to three boys—Daniel, Henry, and Gerrit—and having babies, she discovered, was not nearly as hard as it was said to be. In no time at all she was up and about—not like her mother and so many women who turned themselves into semi-invalids. Of course she had her own ideas about how to take care of babies. She refused to wrap them up tightly in their blankets like cocoons so they couldn't move. Yet this was the custom. Why? she asked. Because their bones were soft, a nurse told her. Nonsense! Elizabeth replied. No one wrapped up baby kittens and they seemed to make out all right with their bones.

Moreover, having babies didn't interfere with her enjoyment of her home. She loved arranging flowers, hanging a batch of clean laundry on the line, and best of all, she liked entertaining. She had many old friends in the area, and she made new ones. It was almost like creating her own Peterboro.

But Henry was not satisfied. He'd do better in New York State, he decided, so in 1847 they moved to Seneca Falls. As it happened (or perhaps didn't just "happen"), Judge Cady owned a house there, which he gave to the Stantons, along with money for Elizabeth to use to fix up the house. Leaving her children in Johnstown with her mother, Elizabeth went ahead, hiring carpenters, painters, paper hangers, glorying in what she called a "full display of my executive ability." She took for granted that she could live happily anywhere, but sometimes she worried about Henry. After all, they were out in the country, two miles from the village of Seneca Falls. The road was not paved; there were no sidewalks, and few people to talk to. Of course they had a nice view of the Seneca River, but there wouldn't be much to their social life. Would Henry become restless?

As it turned out, Elizabeth need not have worried. Henry was not around Seneca Falls long enough to become restless.

He took to traveling, giving antislavery lectures, politicking, taking care of legal business in Albany and New York.

It was Elizabeth who had a hard time. There she was, left with three small mischievous boys and all she had was inexperienced household help, who were no help at all. Either they were too sick to work, too lazy to work, or just didn't know how to work. In order to keep the boys busy, Elizabeth invited neighborhood children over and served cake and milk. She even organized a co-ed gym in the barn for them. She played games and read to the boys when she could steal time from the house, but there wasn't much time. She could barely keep ahead of the chores. Housekeeping was no longer the fun it had been in Boston. She felt as if she were on a treadmill doing the same work over and over again. Cleaning, cooking, washing, sewing. Sometimes she was so frustrated at never having anything finished and done with, she'd call in the carpenter and have him cut out a new window. A window was a once-and-for-all kind of business. Moreover, it looked out at the world, almost as if it were suggesting escape. Henry would just laugh when he came home from a trip. Not another window! he'd say.

Of course Elizabeth looked forward to Henry's homecomings. He always brought presents for the boys and had a romp with them, and it was good to be operating as a family. Still, when Henry wanted to read the paper, he wanted *quiet*. Elizabeth would hush the children, explaining that their father was busy with his daily devotions. When Henry wasn't home, he wrote long letters to Elizabeth, complaining about how lonely he was, begging her to write.

Elizabeth did write, but only one letter to four of his letters.

How could he understand what her life was like? Henry was a man and had been a man for forty-three years. He thought like a man. And men believed that they were the "lords of creation," Elizabeth said. They claimed that the minds of men and women were different, each suited only to its own "sphere." (Men loved the word "sphere." What they really meant was that women should keep in their place, which, of course, was at home.) Men were the wise ones; they made the decisions. Women were the soft, loving ones who were supposed to furnish the comfort. But it was not so, Elizabeth told herself as she swept the kitchen floor. It was not so. Men and women were *not* different. They were created equal, and each should decide his or her own sphere. And hers was certainly not the sphere of household drudgery with no time to read, no friends to talk to, no chance to feel that she, Elizabeth Cady Stanton, was a person in her own right. Lonely and depressed, she suffered, she said, from "mental hunger."

So of course she was delighted on a July day in 1848 to receive an invitation from Lucretia Mott to meet her at Jane Hunt's home in nearby Waterloo, New York. Five women were present—all Quakers (except Elizabeth), all reformers, active in the antislavery cause or the popular temperance movement, which was trying to restrict the use and sale of alcohol. At thirty-two, Elizabeth was the youngest of the group and the most eager. It was almost as if she and Lucretia Mott were at last taking up the conversation they had begun on the steps of the British Museum, but now Elizabeth had had more experience at being a woman. She didn't complain about her own life. What angered her was the general condi-

tion of women who had no say in anything. Not even a say in the government of their own families. A husband was legally allowed to beat his wife. Of course the stick he used was supposed to be no wider than his thumb, but what angry man was going to stop to measure a stick? On the other hand, if the husband came home drunk every night, what could the wife do? Nothing. She couldn't even leave him. The Founding Fathers had talked about "inalienable rights," but what rights did women have?

Elizabeth couldn't have picked a better audience. These were women who were used to taking action when they saw injustice. And the obvious thing to do, they agreed, was to hold a "Woman's Rights Convention." The sooner, the better.

They set the date for July 19 and 20, only five days later. Elizabeth obtained the Wesleyan Chapel in Seneca Falls for the meeting and entered a paragraph in the local paper announcing a "convention to discuss the social, civil, and religious conditions and rights of women." They drew up a declaration of woman's rights and, to give it an air of dignity, they modeled it on the Declaration of Independence. But while the Founding Fathers had talked about the tyranny of King George, he was only *one* man. The women complained of the "tyranny of all men." "The history of mankind," they wrote, "is a history of repeated injuries . . . of man toward woman."

They listed their grievances:

A married woman was treated as if she were civilly dead. She had no right to property, even to the wages she earned.

The divorce laws ignored the happiness of women. Only men had the power to divorce.

A single woman who owned property was taxed, but, since she couldn't vote, this was taxation without representation. Just what had made America rebel against England!

If a woman wanted to work, she had little choice of what she could do. And she wouldn't get much pay.

Women were denied an equal education.

And who decided what woman's "sphere" was? Men, of course. In every way men had tried to destroy a woman's "confidence in her own powers, to lessen her self-respect, and to make her willing to lead a dependent and abject life."

Elizabeth added one more demand, which she said was the most important of all. She wanted women to have the right to vote.

This was a radical idea. Even Lucretia Mott objected. "Lizzie," she said, "thee will make us look ridiculous." People would be so shocked, they'd turn against the convention. Elizabeth was not just suggesting that women should step out of their sphere, she was telling them to *leap* out of it. What could a woman know about politics? people would ask. No decent woman should even want to mix in such sordid business. Henry, who was home, had gone along with the Declaration up to this point, but now he was furious. Elizabeth was going too far. She was embarrassing him, Henry said, and if she insisted, he'd leave town.

But Elizabeth did insist. In the end Lucretia consented. And Henry did exactly what he had threatened to do. He left town. Elizabeth could not have been surprised. He had always been uncomfortable when she showed her independence.

The question was: would people come to their convention? On such short notice, the women were afraid to expect much. It was haying season. How many people would take two days off just to talk about women? As it turned out, many did. On the morning of July 19, both men and women crowded into the chapel at Seneca Falls. Everyone was curious. What were the women up to? Frederick Douglass, the famous ex-slave abolitionist, was there because he wanted to extend freedom wherever he could.

Of course the women who had called the convention were nervous. None of them had ever led a meeting. Suppose they made a mistake and didn't follow the proper rules of order? People would laugh at women who could call a convention but didn't know how to run it. In the end they asked Lucretia's husband, James Mott, to act as chairman. Lucretia spoke first. She told the women in the audience to forget the old rules about not talking. They were *supposed* to talk.

But this was not easy. When it was Elizabeth's turn to talk, even she felt shy. At first her voice could hardly be heard as she read the Declaration of Woman's Rights (or Sentiments, as they preferred to call it), but gradually her voice became stronger. In the end she decided it was exciting to be on stage, standing up in public for what she believed privately.

There were five meetings during the two days of the convention. When at the last meeting a vote was taken on each of the demands in the Declaration, the only one that was opposed was the right of women to vote. But when Frederick Douglass spoke in favor of the voting right, it too passed. A paper was passed around for signatures of all those who supported the Declaration. Sixty-eight women signed; thirty-two men.

When she went home that night, Elizabeth could only

have been happy about the success of the convention. Of course the children and the house were there, waiting for her attention, but they no longer seemed the burden they had been. She had started down her own path. A woman, she would later say, was a woman first, and a wife and mother second. For a while she had lost touch with the woman in her, but now that she'd found her, she could enjoy being a wife and mother.

# CHAPTER FOUR

**E**lizabeth never supposed that a little convention in a small town in upstate New York could make so many people mad. Even people in big cities like New York and Philadelphia. If the women in Seneca Falls had been caught burning the flag or making fun of the Bible, they could hardly have been more viciously attacked. Reporters flung nasty names at them: "sexless old maids," "heretics." What business did women have interfering in the running of the world? "A woman is nobody," a Philadelphia paper declared. "A wife is everything." After all that name-calling, many who had signed the Declaration of Sentiments asked that their names be removed. Harriet Eaton, Elizabeth's own sister, withdrew her name, most likely under pressure from her husband and father.

But if these reporters thought they would discourage Elizabeth Cady Stanton, they were mistaken. All they did was throw obstacles in her way. As if that would stop Elizabeth! As a girl she had jumped her horse over four-foot fences, and she expected to overcome arguments just as well. So whenever she read a criticism, she sat down and answered it. Indeed, these critical reporters gave her a chance to present her ideas on women to a larger audience.

Elizabeth had helped to start a ball rolling, but there were plenty of women ready to roll that ball along. After all, this was an age of reform, and women had already taken part in abolition and temperance movements. Speaking up for woman's rights was a natural next step for them to take. Indeed, another reformer, Lucy Stone, had in 1847 already given the first speech specifically on woman's rights. Just after graduating from Oberlin College, a pioneer college in co-education, she had spoken for woman's rights in her brother's pulpit in Gardner, Massachusetts, and although people admired the "silvery" quality of her voice, she did not receive the widespread attention that the Seneca Falls meeting attracted. Still, on August 2, 1848, when Lucy spoke again at a National Woman's Rights Convention in Worcester, Massachusetts, she was recognized as a leader of the new movement.

More meetings followed in Ohio, Indiana, Massachusetts, Pennsylvania, and New York, but Elizabeth did not feel free to leave her children long enough to attend them. Once when Daniel shot an arrow into Gerrit's eye, all Elizabeth could think was—what if she had been away from home! (Fortunately the injury turned out not to be serious.) So for now Elizabeth stayed home, but she did write letters to be read at the meetings. And in 1849, under the pen name of Sunflower, she began submitting articles to a small temperance magazine, *The Lily,* run by a local woman, Amelia

Bloomer. It wasn't enough, Elizabeth said, for a woman just to talk temperance. If her husband abused her or was habitually drunk, she should have the right to leave him. She should be able to get a divorce. Again her critics were shocked. After all, they said, marriage was "for better or worse," and if a marriage turned out to be worse, a woman should just put up with it. She had promised, hadn't she?

In 1851 there were three important events in Elizabeth's life. First, in January, Elizabeth's cousin Libby Smith (now Libby Miller) came for a visit. Like Elizabeth, Libby was what was called a "woman's righter," and now she had taken a step so bold that she surprised even Elizabeth. There Libby stood on the Stanton doorstep, wearing long trousers topped by a short dress that stopped halfway down her leg. The skirt was full. No petticoat. No corset. A sash at the waist completed an outfit that looked like a Turkish costume. Elizabeth was delighted. About time! she said. She had always complained about how uncomfortable and impractical women's clothes were. You would never catch a man, she said, submitting to whalebones around his waist, or yards of material dragging in the mud.

Elizabeth wasted no time in copying Libby's dress and wearing it. So did a few other women in Seneca Falls, including Amelia Bloomer, who drew a pattern and printed it in her magazine. People had called the new style the "Turkish dress," until Amelia Bloomer advertised it. Then it became known as "bloomers." Bloomers made a great many people mad, but Elizabeth didn't care. She felt as free as a bird let out of its cage. Just look at her! she bragged. Climbing the stairs without holding up her skirts! She could even carry a baby to bed in one arm, and a candle in the other hand. But the male population (and many females as well) were scandalized. Judge Cady asked Elizabeth please not to come to Johnstown in that costume. Elizabeth's sons, Daniel, Henry, and Gerrit, were embarrassed to be seen with her. She couldn't even go into town without boys on the street throwing stones and insulting her. "Breeches! Breeches!" they would shout. Henry, however, knew better than to try to dictate what Elizabeth should wear, but he did tease her about showing off her legs. Some men acted as if women should keep it a secret that they even had legs.

The bloomer uproar didn't die down. "How long," Elizabeth wrote Libby, "will the heathens rage?" After two years the "heathens" were still raging, and Elizabeth, tired of being a laughingstock, went back to conventional clothes. She had important things to say and wanted to be taken seriously. Amelia kept on with the bloomers for seven years; Libby for eight.

The second event happened on February 10, 1851. Elizabeth had a personal announcement to make. She hung a red flag in front of her house because on that day she had given birth to their fourth son, Theodore. If she had had a girl (and she had hoped for one), she would have hung out a white flag. The next year a white flag did go up when Margaret was born. That would be the end of her flags, she believed. Some of the local people thought Mrs. Stanton was putting on airs. What was so special about having a child that you had to proclaim it as if it were a national holiday? Henry apparently didn't think a new child was special. He was serving a two-year term as state senator and did not come home for Theo-

dore's arrival. But then Henry was not at home when any of the children were born. Indeed, during the 1850s he would come and go, but he was away from home on an average of ten months each year.

Also in 1851 a new friend came into Elizabeth Stanton's life. Susan B. Anthony, a tall, plain, intense woman, turned out to be not only a friend to Elizabeth, but also a lifelong partner in her work. Susan was a single woman with a Quaker background who lived in Rochester. Her first introduction to Elizabeth was on a street corner in Seneca Falls. Susan was visiting Amelia Bloomer; Elizabeth was returning from an abolition meeting, and she was in a hurry. William Lloyd Garrison was coming for dinner and Elizabeth's mind was in her kitchen. Later, when Elizabeth and Susan became good friends, they would laugh about that first street-corner meeting.

Still, these two women did come to know each other and, before long, each realized that she needed the other. Both were devoted to the cause of woman's rights, and although Susan had been involved with the temperance movement, Elizabeth convinced her that they had "bigger fish to fry." Right away they could see that they had different talents. Susan was painstaking, deliberate, untiring; Elizabeth was quick, daring, charismatic, and she had a way with words. They worked well together. Moreover, they liked each other and needed the kind of boost each was able to give the other's morale.

"I long to see you," Elizabeth once wrote. If she could see Susan once a week, she said, it would raise her "self-esteem."

In her turn Susan said, "Mrs. Stanton, I have *very weak*

moments . . . and I feel *alone*. . . . Don't fail to write me. It always does me so much good to get a letter from you." (No matter how long Susan knew Elizabeth, she called her "Mrs. Stanton.")

Elizabeth and Susan forged one of those rare friendships that was at the center of their lives. Susan B. Anthony, hampered by no domestic duties of her own, prodded Elizabeth to take on more work, to attend more meetings, to step more to the forefront of the movement. Elizabeth, frustrated by the limitations of her life, would occasionally let off steam in her letters.

"Men and angels, give me patience!" she once exclaimed. "I am at the boiling point! How much I long to be free of housekeeping and children so as to have time to think and read and write."

Actually, it was no wonder that Elizabeth called on "men and angels" for patience. She was at her wit's end with the children, particularly with her three older boys—Daniel, ten years old in 1852, Henry, eight, and Gerrit, seven. Elizabeth had always given them more freedom than most children had, letting them stay in bed in the morning until they were ready to get up, not requiring that they go to church, often bribing them to obey. Now they were completely out of control. Neighbors were constantly complaining that they threw stones at their windows. But they didn't stick to the usual mischief. They liked to experiment. Once they undressed young Theodore when he was little more than a year old, tied a string of corks around him, and put him in the Seneca River to see if he would float. (He did.) Again the boys hauled Theodore up to the roof, sat him against the chimney, and left him there. Luckily, he was rescued before he came to any harm. News of such exploits must have reached Judge Cady, for he wrote to Henry, advising him to go home and take a hand with his sons. Before long the two older boys were sent away to a private school in New Jersey.

Often Susan came to the rescue. She would come down to Seneca Falls and take care of the children and "stir the pudding" while Elizabeth wrote a speech for Susan to deliver. Henry used to say that Susan stirred the pudding, Elizabeth stirred up Susan, and Susan stirred up the world. Certainly Susan felt at home in the Stanton household. The children called her "Aunt Susan," although they were a little afraid of her. One of Susan's eyes was crossed and didn't seem to move when the other eye did, so they suspected that she could see around corners and spy on them.

Further relief from housework came when Elizabeth found Amelia Willard, a competent, caring woman who stayed with the family for thirty-one years. But Elizabeth's daughter, Margaret, was still a baby, and Elizabeth always refused to leave the children in their first years. She planned, however, for Margaret to be the last child, and Susan knew this. Indeed, they both looked forward to the time when Elizabeth would be free. Still, Susan prodded her to do more. Elizabeth laughed. If Susan nagged too much, she teased, she would have another baby.

# CHAPTER FIVE

Margaret was younger than two years old when Elizabeth was asked by the women's association in New York to address the New York State Legislature in Albany. For once the women wanted to speak directly to the men who made the laws. And who could present their case better than Elizabeth Cady Stanton?

The very idea was scary. For a woman to speak to an audience of men was hard enough, but to speak to the men who governed the state of New York! The men who made the laws in her father's law books! This would be the highest fence that Elizabeth had ever tried to jump over. But she was thirty-eight years old and she had held herself back too long. Of course she would do it. She would take Amelia Willard and the three youngest children, put them up in an Albany hotel while she took on what she called the "great event" of her life. She enlisted the help of Susan, and for two months, she worked on her speech. She knew she must argue as logically as a man and prove that women were capable of taking part in the political process.

When Judge Cady read in the newspaper what Elizabeth planned to do, he was shocked. He knew that she was independent, but now she was making a public display of herself! He asked her to stop in Johnstown on her way to Albany. If he heard the speech, perhaps he could persuade her to give up the idea. In any case, Elizabeth went into her father's study and read the speech aloud to what she knew was the most critical audience she ever would have.

There are various versions as to how this interview ended. In her autobiography Elizabeth described her father as sympathetic and helpful, but Elizabeth was never willing to criticize her husband or her father in print. Her later letters to Susan, however, indicate how deeply distressed she was by her father's continued opposition. Being as good as a boy or a man was not what Judge Cady wanted. He had never wanted it, and he didn't now. Of course Elizabeth knew this, but again she was hurt, as hurt as she'd ever been.

She left for Albany. On February 14, 1854, the day of her big event, Elizabeth put on a black silk dress with a white lace collar and fastened a diamond pin at her throat. She mounted the platform of the Senate chamber and looked into the audience. Not a single member of her family was there to support her. But Susan was there. Dear, loyal Susan.

Elizabeth spoke with authority. She listed all the rights that women were denied. Above all, she argued, women must be

given the right to vote. She was eloquent, and although she was praised for her performance, as usual she was also criticized. An Albany newspaper referred to her as "one of those unsexed women who would step out of their true sphere." (Privately she referred to the Albany editors as men with heads the size of apples.)

As she made plans for her future, Judge Cady continued to badger her about her public appearances. Did she plan to continue lecturing? he asked. Yes, Elizabeth replied, she did.

"Your first lecture," Judge Cady said, "will be a very expensive one."

Elizabeth understood exactly what her father was saying. He was threatening to cut her out of his will. She didn't flinch. "I intend that it shall be a very profitable one."

When it was clear that Elizabeth would not back down from her campaign, her whole family lined up against her. Even Henry. Elizabeth did not find it easy to throw off her family's opposition.

"I passed through a terrible scourging when last at my father's," she wrote Susan. "I cannot tell you how deep the iron entered my soul. To think that all in me of which my father would have felt a proper pride had I been a man is deeply mortifying to him because I am a woman. But," she added, "I will both write and speak."

Still, for a while she did stay close to home. She concentrated on writing and looked forward to the day when she could do what she wanted. She never supposed that anything would upset her plans, yet in January 1856, another baby arrived. Up went the white flag in honor of Harriot Eaton Stanton. As much as Elizabeth loved her children, she couldn't help but be disappointed in this interruption of her plans. "I might have been born an orator before spring," she wrote Susan.

Susan's reaction was stronger. Everyone was deserting her! She had felt betrayed when two leaders in the movement, Lucy Stone and Antoinette Brown, married the previous year, each to a Blackwell brother. Lucy had done something unheard-of; she had kept her maiden name. Although this shocked many people, even those in the movement, Susan was upset that Lucy had married at all. She and Lucy didn't have time for such "personal matters," Susan scolded.

And now these women were having babies! Suppose she too fell by the wayside and married? Susan asked Elizabeth. Then what would happen? Since there was no one on the horizon who seemed inclined to marry Susan, Elizabeth did not worry. She simply continued to read Susan's complaints.

"Those of you who have the *talent* to do honor to poor—

oh! how poor—womanhood," Susan moaned, "have all given yourself over to baby making; and left poor brainless me to do battle alone." And here she was, Susan wailed, scheduled to address a teachers' convention and not a word written! "Don't delay one mail," she begged, "to tell me what you *will do*."

Elizabeth answered promptly. "Your servant is not dead, but liveth." She would do what she could.

The following year (August 1857) Elizabeth tried to encourage Susan: "You and I have a prospect of a good long life. We shall not be in our prime before fifty, and after that we shall be good for twenty years at least." Only two or three more years, she promised Susan, before they'd be in the "battlefield" together.

But the battle, Susan reported, was not going well. She was discouraged. She doubted if men would ever change, she wrote Elizabeth. They were born convinced that they were mentally superior. They were born knowing that they were *meant* to rule. It would take centuries, she said, to persuade them to give up this fancy. "God and angels keep you safe from all hindrances. If you come not to the rescue, who shall?"

Elizabeth may not have realized that a hindrance already lay in her path, or perhaps she didn't have the heart to tell Susan. Yes, she was expecting another baby. A seventh. When Susan was finally told, she wrote in a frenzy to Antoinette Brown Blackwell. Mrs. Stanton had done it again. "Ah me!!! Alas!! Alas!!!! Mrs. Stanton!!" she wrote. "Her husband, you know, does not *help* to make it easy for her to engage in such work, and all her friends throw *mountains* in her path. Mr. Stanton will be gone most of the autumn, full of *Political Air Castles*. The whole burden of home and children, therefore, falls to her. But there is no remedy now."

On March 13, 1859, a red flag went up. Robert Livingston Stanton arrived, the one baby who from the beginning had given Elizabeth trouble. Her recovery was so slow that four weeks later she wrote Susan that she was still unable to walk across the room: "You need expect nothing from me for some time."

The rest of the year went badly for Elizabeth. And for the country as well. In October, John Brown, a militant abolitionist who wanted to arm the slaves, seized the United States arsenal at Harpers Ferry, Virginia. Since he had the help of only a very few men, he didn't hold the arsenal long, but the news rocked the nation. From day to day people followed the story of John Brown's capture, his arrest, and finally (on December 2) his hanging. Elizabeth didn't just read the story as if it were happening far away in Virginia. This story touched her family. John Brown was a close friend of Gerrit Smith's. Moreover, his raid was said to have been planned at the Smiths' Peterboro home. And Gerrit was supposedly one of the "Secret Six" who had financed the raid. What was more, John Brown's wife had sought refuge in Lucretia Mott's home.

Elizabeth suffered for her cousin Gerrit. Here he was, partly responsible for the death of his close friend, a man whom the abolitionists idolized. And indeed, Gerrit Smith was so upset that he broke down completely and was committed to an insane asylum. As far as Elizabeth was concerned, this was a fate "worse than death." At the time she couldn't know that this was a nervous breakdown from which he'd soon recover.

In the midst of this trouble Elizabeth's father died. Elizabeth had stayed away from Johnstown since their last quarrel, and now it was too late to smooth over the rough words between them. "No, no, no," the church bells tolled. Elizabeth's father would never forgive her; no, never accept her; no, never even speak to her again. And she would never hear the words she had so longed to hear.

But in spite of his threat, Judge Cady had not legally disowned her. In his will he had left her, just as he had left her sisters, $50,000. This would not have lessened Elizabeth's grief, but it did make it easier for her to find her freedom. And find it, she did. Her mother helped by opening her house to Elizabeth's children. Elizabeth could leave the youngest ones in Johnstown for an entire summer if she chose, or for shorter periods if she went lecturing. Elizabeth had always admired her mother (in spite of those early no's), but with her father gone, her mother seemed to feel free to offer a closer friendship.

# CHAPTER SIX

Elizabeth had waited through seven babies to be "born an orator," but in 1860 she was at last ready. It was a good year for orators, an election year when a new president would be chosen. The question was: would he be a slavery man or an antislavery man? He better not be antislavery, southerners warned. They would quit the Union before they'd let an antislavery man rule them. Elizabeth had no notion of lecturing on politics, but she could do what Lucretia Mott was doing—lecture on slavery. Indeed, more and more she was lumping women and slaves together when she talked.

"To you, white man," she declared in one speech, "the world throws open wide her gates . . . but the black man and the woman are born to shame."

On November 6, 1860, Abraham Lincoln was elected to the presidency. Southerners branded him antislavery and they did exactly what they had threatened to do. In December, South Carolina seceded from the Union, followed quickly by

other states. Many abolitionists in the North were also dissat-
isfied with Lincoln. How strong was he against slavery? True,
he had said, "A house divided against itself cannot stand." He
was opposed to slavery being introduced to new territories.
On the other hand, he had pledged to uphold the Fugitive
Slave Law, which required that escaped slaves be returned to
their owners in the South. Northerners despised this law and
so were suspicious of Lincoln. Furthermore, he wasn't making any promises to emancipate slaves. Perhaps he wouldn't.
So why not step up the movement for emancipation before
Lincoln was inaugurated in March?

The abolitionists went to work, holding meetings, handing
out petitions. Elizabeth and Susan were assigned to cover
New York State. From town to town Elizabeth went, but she
might as well have stayed home. No one would listen to her.
People thought abolitionists wanted war, and they didn't
want to hear any more of their talk. Still, they came to her
meetings. They came in mobs, rowdy disorderly mobs. When
she began to speak, they drowned her out, hissing, booing,
heckling. In only one place was Elizabeth permitted to have
her say. In Albany the mayor sat on the stage beside her, a
revolver on his knee.

Henry wrote to her: "I think you risk your lives. . . . [The]
mobcrats would as soon kill you as not." He advised her to
go home. And she did.

Elizabeth remembered the winter of 1861 as "the winter of
mobs." Sick of Seneca Falls, she longed for a change. So when
Henry was given a minor job as deputy collector of customs
in New York City, Elizabeth quickly packed up and moved
the family there to join him. She was forty-six years old and

had lived upstate long enough. Now she would be where the action was.

And once Lincoln took office, the pace of life picked up in a frightening way. War was declared. Susan was a pacifist, so she was against war. Any war for any reason. But not Elizabeth. The war was "music to my ears," she said. If it took a war to secure freedom, let it come—the sooner the better. And if her sons wanted to join up, she'd be proud. Daniel, who had no desire to go to war, went to work for his father, but eighteen-year-old Henry ran away and enlisted. The younger boys drilled every day in the gymnasium, and Elizabeth basked in the glory of being "one of mothers of the Republic." Besides, when the slaves got their freedom, she figured, women would get theirs too. The government couldn't dole out equality in bits and pieces. "Equality" meant "equality for all."

She expected emancipation to be declared right away. But Lincoln didn't even talk about emancipation. All he talked about was preserving the Union.

Months went by. What was the matter with the man? abolitionists asked. Still, he made no announcement.

At last on January 1, 1863, Lincoln did issue the Emancipation Proclamation, but according to the abolitionists, it was not enough. Only the slaves in those states still in active rebellion against the North were freed. Like other abolitionists, Elizabeth and Susan wanted *all* slaves freed.

So they sent petitions out over the country, asking that emancipation be extended in a constitutional amendment to apply to all slaves. For months the signed petitions poured in. Elizabeth's three older boys helped tie up the petitions, mark the state they represented, and note the number of signatures included. By August 1864 there were 400,000 names.

On April 9, 1865, the war ended and soon after, the Thirteenth Amendment, freeing all slaves, was passed. The question now was: what was the status of the freed slaves? Were they to be granted all the rights of citizens? Could they vote?

The abolitionists agreed that yes, in new amendments Negroes should be given the same rights as other citizens. But women should also have those rights, Elizabeth insisted. The government could not recognize blacks and ignore women.

But it could. Newspapers talked of women asking for their rights now as a lot of "tomfoolery." The men insisted that this was "the Negro's hour," and women would have their turn later. Just wait, they said. If woman's rights were considered now, the Negro's rights would be endangered.

Did the government not think that some of the Negroes were women? Elizabeth asked.

Later, the Fourteenth Amendment said that all persons born or naturalized in the United States were citizens. Then it went on to say that states had to let all *male* citizens vote. Elizabeth was infuriated by the word "male." Had it not been for that one word, women would have been legally eligible citizens too. The Fifteenth Amendment was more specific about Negroes. It declared that the right of citizens to vote shall not be denied "on account of race, color, or previous condition of servitude." Still, not one word about women! Elizabeth wrote to Susan who was visiting in Kansas: "Come back and help."

More petitions were sent to Congress (10,000 in all), insisting that no one should be kept from voting on account of *race or sex.* How could educated women be denied the vote, Elizabeth asked, while illiterate black men could step right up to the polls? Leaders whom she had always trusted, men like Gerrit Smith, told Elizabeth to be patient. Patient! Men and angels! What else had she been?

It was a long process to get a constitutional amendment ratified by all the states, and Elizabeth was not going to hang around, just waiting. Why not run for office? she asked herself. She might not be able to vote, but there was not one word in the constitution to prevent men from voting *for* her. She didn't expect to be elected, but if she ran, that in itself would be something. So in 1866 she put herself up as an independent candidate for Congress from the 8th District of New York. Out of 2,300 votes, she got only 24, but she was proud of every one of those.

Elizabeth was fifty-one years old now, one year into her "prime," when, she had promised Susan, they would go into the battlefield together. In 1867 she got her chance. Kansas was considering two amendments to its state constitution. One was for Negro suffrage and one was for woman suffrage. (The term "suffrage," meaning the right to vote, had come into usage during the war.)

So off Elizabeth and Susan went. By train to Kansas and then across the state any way they could. Danger didn't matter; difficulty was to be expected; surprises were routine. After all, this was the West! And Elizabeth loved it: the never-ending open space, the huge sky, even the hardships.

In order to cover more territory, Susan and Elizabeth separated. Charles Robinson, the former governor of Kansas, accompanied Elizabeth, traveling in a mule-drawn carriage over rough country, stopping wherever they could gather an audience. Elizabeth spoke in log cabins, schools, churches, hotels, barns, and in the open air. Often they traveled at night in such pitch blackness that the governor had to walk ahead of the carriage in his white shirt sleeves so Elizabeth could see him, while she drove the mules. Across streams, down one side of a canyon, up the other. But the greatest test for Elizabeth came when the day's traveling was done. Whenever a log cabin turned up at the right time, they would ask if they could stay. The answer was always a welcoming yes, and Elizabeth would be offered a bed, while the owner of the bed and the governor took to the floor.

This was what Elizabeth dreaded. The bed! The idea that sheets could be washed had apparently not reached Kansas. Nor that beds were not meant to be shared with bedbugs— swarms of them. Generally Elizabeth went to bed with her clothes on, but clothes were no protection. Once she thought she felt something more than a bedbug run across her head. Perhaps a mouse.

Asked if she was comfortable, Elizabeth mentioned the mouse.

"I should not wonder," came the reply. "I have heard such squeaking the past week, I told Sister there must be a mouse nest in that bed."

One night she decided to give the governor the bed while she slept in the carriage. For once, she figured, she would have an undisturbed rest. Free from bedbugs. Free from mice. But not, as it turned out, free from pigs. Long-nosed black pigs crowded around the carriage, snorting and scratching

themselves noisily against the iron steps. Elizabeth picked up the whip, flicked it to one side of the carriage, then to the other. All night she flicked but she never drove the pigs away.

Still, in spite of the discomforts, Elizabeth reveled in the experience. She was proud of her endurance and her ability to cope. No matter what anyone said or didn't say, she really was as good as a man. The morning after a bad night, she and the governor would laugh about all they had put up with.

There were real obstacles, however, that could not be laughed off. Money, for instance. They were running out of it. And opposition. She didn't expect help from the Democrats; they had always been against black freedom, but Republicans might have stepped forward. But no, back East, Republicans were raising the old cry: it was the Negro's hour. Let the women wait. This was a blow to Elizabeth. Some of her best friends in the abolition movement opposed her. So when a rich Democrat appeared out of the blue and offered to help the women, how could Elizabeth and Susan say no?

Tall, handsome, dressed in a blue coat with brass buttons, patent leather boots, and lavender gloves, George Francis Train not only made his money available for the cause, but for two weeks he spoke in behalf of woman suffrage. "Every man in Kansas," he said, "who throws a vote for the Negro and not for women, has insulted his mother, his daughter, his sister, and his wife."

He was a good entertainer. Once, in a scene he created on stage, he played the part of a worn-out wife, bending over a washtub when her husband (Mr. Train taking both parts) reeled into the room, drunk as an owl. When the tour was over, he chartered a special train and accompanied Elizabeth and Susan back to New York. Moreover, he gave them money to run a magazine devoted to woman suffrage.

Mr. Train, however, was not popular with Elizabeth's and Susan's friends. Governor Robinson called him an "egotistical clown." Many thought he was a fraud. Lucy Stone, as well as others in the movement, could not understand how Elizabeth and Susan could be taken in by such a man. "He was a lunatic," Lucy said, "wild and ranting. He made the cause a laughingstock everywhere." But who else, Elizabeth asked, would have given them money for a magazine?

They called the magazine *The Revolution*. And that was another mistake, they were told. The opposition had always claimed that women were trying to make a revolution, and now they themselves were admitting it.

Elizabeth laughed. What should they have called their paper? she asked. *The Rosebud*?

In any case, the magazine didn't last long. George Francis Train went to Ireland, was jailed for radical activities, and withdrew his support. As for Kansas, it voted against both Negro suffrage and woman suffrage. And the Fifteenth Amendment was ratified without a single reference to women.

Still, Elizabeth was glad that she'd had her Kansas adventure.

# CHAPTER SEVEN

**I**n the spring of 1868 Elizabeth bought a house in Tenafly, New Jersey. She had tried the experiment of living full-time with Henry and had decided that they both did better on the old Seneca Falls come-and-go schedule. Henry too, apparently, was tired of around-the-clock matrimony in New York, and preferred an arrangement that allowed him to visit his family. A friend once said that Henry needed a "humble companion" who would share *his* interests. But so did Elizabeth. Someone like James Mott, who would sit in the audience when Lucretia spoke, and hold her bonnet.

And right now Elizabeth needed support. Strong abolitionists, like Gerrit Smith and Lucy Stone, resented the fact that she opposed the Fifteenth Amendment just because it didn't include women. Many disapproved of her friendship with George Francis Train of the lavender gloves, and were shocked at her ideas about marriage and divorce. Elizabeth, however, did not intend to trim her sails. No one who wanted to bring about reform, she said, could tiptoe around, worrying about what others thought. "Those who are really in earnest must be willing to be anything or nothing in the world's estimation . . . and bear the consequences."

In 1869 there was a consequence. The women's movement split in two. Elizabeth and Susan formed the National Woman Suffrage Association, which refused to admit men as members. In Boston Lucy Stone headed the more conservative American Woman Suffrage Association, whose members included both men and women. Lucretia tried her best to make peace between the two groups, but she spent more time with the "old pioneers"—Elizabeth and Susan. And all the time she urged Elizabeth to write a history of the women's movement.

But Elizabeth didn't want to sit down and review old history. She wanted to act on her own, say what she wanted, and be independent, as she had been during her Kansas trip. So when she was invited to participate in a series of paid lectures, she readily agreed. For eight months each year for the next ten years (1869 to 1879), Elizabeth traveled from city to city on the lecture circuit, speaking on woman's rights, staying at hotels which might, as she said, be "despicable," but whose beds at least were better than log-cabin beds. Her three oldest children (Daniel, Henry, and Gerrit) were grown and out of the house, and she left the others (Robert, the youngest, was eleven) in the care of Amelia. Henry could occasionally come out from the city to oversee the household. It was time that he took his turn.

Elizabeth spent so much time on trains during these years that she didn't hesitate to arrange everything for her comfort.

A great believer in fresh air, she marched through railway cars, propping open the ventilators, shutting the dampers of the stoves, and at the same time making friends right and left. She was so jolly and outgoing that people generally let her do what she wanted. Indeed, it was hard for strangers to believe that this plump, motherly lady with the white hair was the radical Mrs. Stanton. She looked more like the mother of a president, perhaps George Washington. And it was something of a shock to see George Washington's mother playing cards with army officers, as Elizabeth once did, all across the state of Texas. A minister traveling in the same car took Elizabeth to task. How could a respectable, white-haired lady allow herself to be seen playing cards? he asked. And with army men! Elizabeth said she loved games and that was that.

From Maine to California she traveled, introducing fresh air wherever she went, handing out pamphlets. But not everyone received her pamphlets. Elizabeth knew it would be a waste to give a pamphlet to any man with an apple-sized head and high heels on his boots. And to any woman who had what Elizabeth called a "prunes and prism" face. A prune-faced woman would only toss her head and say she had all the rights she wanted, thank you. Elizabeth had become an expert in sizing up people.

Once after a pro-suffrage lecture, a man commented, "My wife has presented me with eight beautiful children; is not this a better life work than exercising the right of suffrage?"

Another apple-headed man! "I have met few men in my life," Elizabeth replied evenly, "worth repeating eight times."

She heard the old arguments again and again.

Would it not seem indelicate for a woman to enter a man's world and be exposed to the realities there?

Many men, Elizabeth pointed out, especially if they were drinking men, exposed their wives regularly to harsh realities on their own hearthstones.

But how could housekeeping and voting be combined? women asked.

Why not? Elizabeth asked. The country would be better off if it had good housekeeping applied to it.

Still, did Mrs. Stanton not think it would be a physical hardship for women to vote?

Not at all, Elizabeth replied. If a woman could carry a twenty-pound child about, she should be able to drop a little piece of paper into a box.

Eighteen seventy-two was another election year, but Elizabeth did not allow politics to interrupt her tour. Still, she followed the activities with interest. Susan was working hard to persuade the Republican party to include a plank in its platform that would support woman suffrage. The Republicans would say only that they were "mindful" of their obligations to the loyal women of America and would listen to their demands "with respect." Susan seemed to welcome the statement, but not Elizabeth. This wasn't a "plank," she scoffed. It was only a "splinter"—no more than a "toothpick." At election time she was still out West when Susan decided to put the Fourteenth Amendment to a test. If all persons born in the United States were citizens, as the amendment stated, she was a citizen. So why not just go ahead, register, and vote? On Election Day, November 5, Susan, along with fourteen other women of the Rochester area, actually voted. "Well,"

Susan wrote Elizabeth, "I have been and gone and done it, positively voted this morning at seven o'clock."

This was headline news all over the country, and of course it was Susan B. Anthony's name that was featured.

On November 18, Susan and the other fourteen were arrested and the trial set for June 17. It was not a normal trial, not even a fair one. The judge was going to make absolutely sure that the trial came out as he wanted, so he didn't allow the jurors to say one word, nor even discuss the case. Instead he ordered them to bring in an immediate verdict of guilty. Then he dismissed them. Susan was fined $100, but when she refused to pay, the judge let her go. He didn't want her money; he had what he wanted. President Grant eventually pardoned the women, but as far as Susan was concerned, she needed no pardon. She had done nothing wrong.

If some women still were not convinced that the Fourteenth Amendment allowed them to vote, the question was settled once and for all in 1875 by the Supreme Court. Considering a similar case, the Court ruled that voting was not an automatic *right* of all citizens, but a *privilege* that the states granted to those it deemed fit.

There was only one thing to do. The women would have to seek a new amendment for themselves. In 1878 they were ready. They had started off their campaign with their old petition strategy, and when they had gathered 10,000 names, they went to the Senate and presented each senator with the names collected from his state.

The senators did not take the petitions or the women seriously. Indeed, they appeared to consider them a huge joke. A reporter described the scene: "The entire Senate presented the appearance of a laughing-school practicing side-splitting and ear-extended grins."

Nevertheless, there were a half dozen or more senators who did support the women. One of them arranged for Elizabeth Cady Stanton to speak on the proposed Sixteenth Amendment before the Senate Committee on Privileges and Elections. Elizabeth was sixty-three years old now, a veteran orator, accustomed to opposition. What she got from this audience, however, was worse than opposition, worse even than laughter.

The committee would not listen. Indeed, the chairman, according to Elizabeth, "took special pains not to listen. He alternately looked over newspapers, then jumped up to open or close a door or window. He stretched, yawned, gazed at the ceiling, cut his nails, sharpened his pencil, changing his occupation every two minutes."

Long ago Elizabeth had said that women would never win their freedom until they became mad enough to swear. Well, men and angels! She was so mad, she felt like hurling her speech at the chairman's head. But then she was in a state of "chronic rebellion." It would serve men right, she once said, if women would go on strike—quit ironing their husbands' shirts, quit doing housework, until they had been given the vote.

After this disastrous meeting with the Senate, Elizabeth continued to fill her speaking engagements. But by 1879 she had had enough of touring. What had once seemed like an adventure was now just an exhausting routine. She was sick of smiling and looking intelligent and interested, she wrote Libby Miller, when she felt like a "squeezed sponge." She had always contended that one reason she kept up her heavy schedule was to make money to send her children to college. But with all her children older than twenty now, she experienced a new sense of freedom. She would go home and do as she pleased. She would spend more time with her grown children, whose company she enjoyed more and more.

In 1880, Elizabeth described an evening together in Tenafly. "Maggie and Bob are playing delightfully on the piano and the violin," she wrote. "Theodore is out taking his evening walk; Hattie reading; Henry [Jr.] and Neil [Daniel] are smoking on the piazza, and Bruno [their English sheep dog] barking at passers-by." Only Henry, Sr., and Gerrit were missing, but Henry was often there. Elizabeth had had the veranda screened so he could smoke his pipe and muse unmolested.

Two years before, Margaret, attended by Vassar classmates, was married under "the old familiar oaks" at Tenafly. It was a beautiful wedding, but it was Bruno who stole the show. At the end of the wedding procession he took his place, bringing up the rear, marching in a stately manner. When the procession stopped, Bruno stopped. He sat at attention, turning his head this way and that as if he were following the vows.

Daniel, who had been the problem child, was his mother's favorite. He spent much of his time in the city with his father, but when he knew Elizabeth was alone at Tenafly, he would go out and get her to read to him. He liked her undivided attention. He married in his forties, moved to Iowa, had one daughter, divorced his wife, and died at the age of forty-eight, leaving his entire estate to his mother.

Gerrit also moved to Iowa, married, and hung portraits of

his mother and Susan B. Anthony over his sofa. Henry, Jr., did not marry until he was forty-eight, and had no children. Bob, the youngest son, never married.

Theodore and Harriot were the reformers. Harriot showed her spirit of independence early. When she was a little girl her father once told her to come down from a high tree limb, but she replied, "Tell Bob. He's three years younger and one branch higher." Later Harriot would take up the cause of women where Elizabeth left off.

# CHAPTER EIGHT

Eighteen eighty was again a year of political conventions, and again Susan attempted to get one or both political parties to make a commitment to women in their platforms. Elizabeth knew that the Democrats were hopeless, and she had little faith in the Republicans. She thought women had "sat on the limb of the Republican tree singing 'Suffrage, if you please,' long enough." Still, she did write out some statements for Susan to use. But for what? Not even a toothpick in the platform this year.

In the fall of 1880, Lucretia Mott died. Elizabeth delivered a eulogy at the next meeting of the National Association, but more important, she felt she could no longer postpone the job that Lucretia had been begging her to do. She would sit down now and write a history of woman suffrage. So she and Susan and their longtime ally, Mathilda Jocelyn Gage, signed a paper of partnership and went to work. Susan came to Tenafly, but she hated the work. Here she was, just sitting around, going over old times, when she wanted to be out and doing. Nevertheless, week after week, she pored over old correspondence and clippings, while Elizabeth wrote up the narrative. Elizabeth later described them at a big table, surrounded by books and papers, "laughing, talking, squabbling day in and out." And eating. Susan cooked her specialty—apple tapioca pudding, and Elizabeth produced her favorites, squash pie and orange cake. Elizabeth undoubtedly ate too much, for she was no longer pleasingly plump; she was downright fat—very fat. Susan scolded her, but it did no good.

Sometimes people asked them how they could write a history of woman suffrage before suffrage had even been attained. They didn't expect to write it *all*, Elizabeth said, but only as far as they'd gone. Still, she had no doubt that someone else would complete it. Not in her lifetime, perhaps. She had accepted that, but she knew that the time would come. "We are only the stone that started the ripple," she said. But the history of that stone took up three large volumes.

One day in the midst of their work, the doorbell rang, and there stood a representative of the Republican party. It was Election Day, and he wondered if anyone in the house needed a ride to the polls. On the spur of the moment, Elizabeth spoke up. Yes, she would like a ride. She was three times the voting age, she said, had lived thirteen years in Tenafly, paid taxes, was a citizen, so of course she planned to vote. She knew, of course, the Supreme Court's decision. She knew of Susan's attempt to vote eight years earlier. Indeed, she may have been a bit jealous of Susan, who had done just the kind of thing that Elizabeth would have liked to do. In any case, Elizabeth stepped into the carriage, and Susan went with her.

She did not, however, make as big a splash as Susan had. Two of the inspectors pulled their hats down over their eyes when they saw her, and pretended that they weren't there. The third put his arms around the ballot box and covered up the slit for the ballot. Only men could vote, he said. Elizabeth flung her ballot in his direction and stamped out as if she had really done something. Well, she had shocked the inspectors, and perhaps the people of Tenafly too. At least she thought so. "The whole town is agape with my act," she bragged.

Elizabeth took time out from writing to make two trips to Europe, the first in 1882 when the first two volumes were completed, the second in 1886 when the third volume was done. The sea trip itself was no longer the pleasant experience it once had been. She didn't get seasick, but on her way to Europe she found her bunk so narrow, she couldn't move at all. It was like sleeping in a coffin, she said. The next day an extension was built on to her bunk, but still she felt cramped. From then on, she endured the trip only because she could be with her daughter Harriot (Harriot Blatch, now), who lived in England. An even greater attraction was Harriot's little Nora, who called her grandmother "Queen Mother."

While Elizabeth was in England, Henry died. Standing in the rain on election night, he caught a cold, developed pneumonia, and died on January 14, 1887. Although they no longer shared what Elizabeth called "the joy of deep soul-love," she did still care for him. She regretted, however, that for so many years she had been without a man "to reverence and worship as a god." For a woman who preached the equality of the sexes, this was a strange admission to make, but she had always wanted more from her father and her husband than they had been able to give.

Back in America, Susan was taking another step forward for woman suffrage. The question of suffrage actually reached the Senate floor in 1887 and was debated. Every year since the proposed Sixteenth Amendment or Woman's Rights Amendment had first been formulated, Susan had reintroduced it. Referred to now as the Susan B. Anthony Amendment, it had never been taken seriously enough to be considered by the entire Senate. This time the suffragists presented the signatures of 200,000 women in favor of the amendment, while 200 preachers and the president of Harvard University were against it. Apparently the preachers' word had more weight. When the vote was taken, thirty-four senators voted no, sixteen senators voted yes, and twenty-six senators preferred not to commit themselves. So Susan would simply have to trundle that old amendment back to the Senate the next year. And the next, and the next.

Elizabeth knew that her time in England was limited. She would have to be back by March 1888, when she and Susan had planned what would be their most ambitious project. They were going to host an International Council of Women, which would take place in the same year they celebrated the fortieth anniversary of the Seneca Falls meeting. Susan had invited all the "pioneers," those who had signed the original Declaration, and she was hoping that many foreign countries would send delegates. Of course, Elizabeth would have a leading role. She had agreed to deliver both the opening and closing speeches, but as the time approached, she didn't see how she could go. How could she bear to leave Nora? How could she face that dreadful ocean voyage? She wrote Susan. Maybe she wouldn't come, after all.

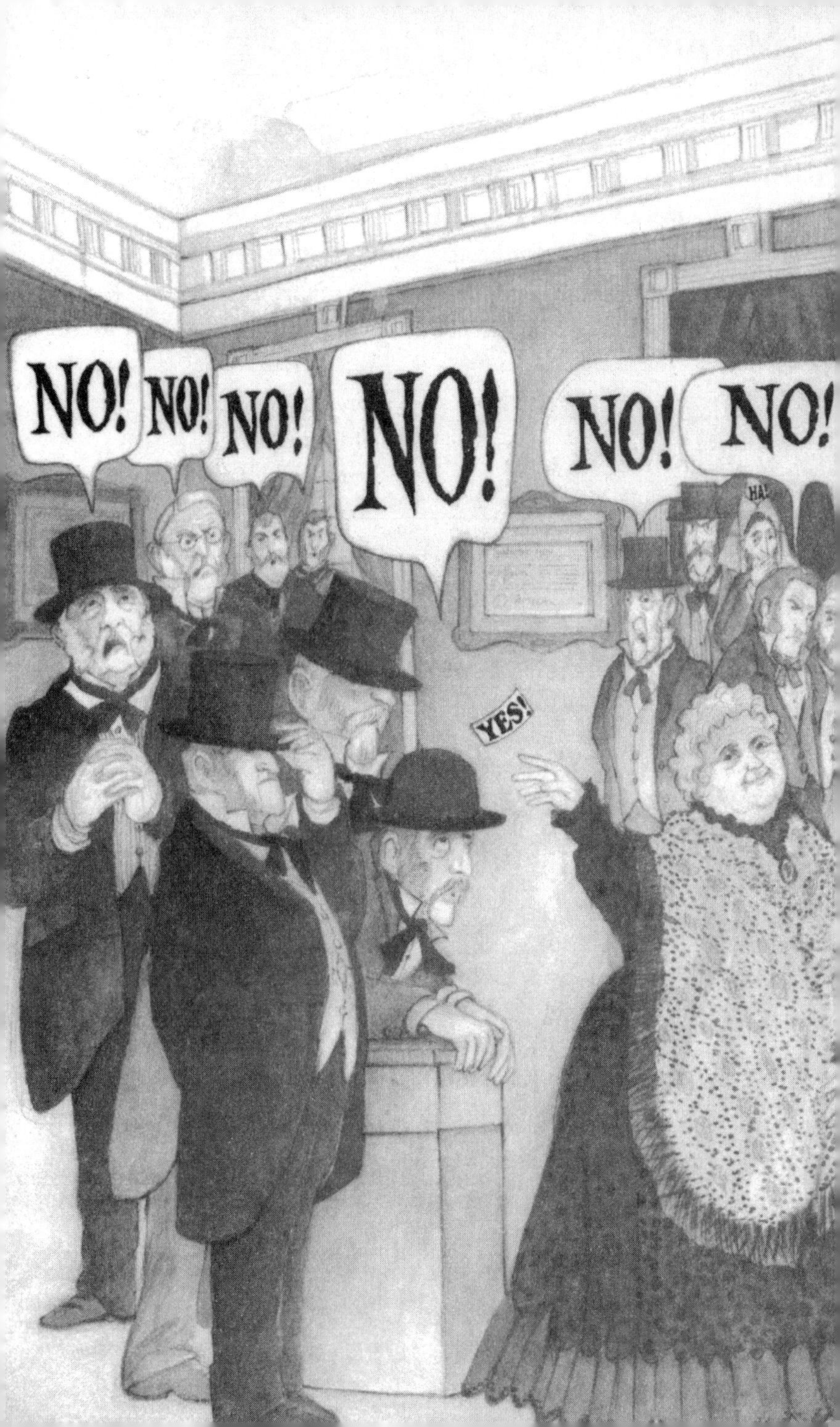
NO!
NO!
NO!
NO!
NO!
NO!
YES!

Susan was furious. What was Elizabeth thinking? How could she not come to the anniversary of a movement that she had helped to start? Susan wrote such a blistering letter that she said "it would start every white hair on her head." Libby Miller wrote too.

Elizabeth wired back: "I am coming."

She arrived in the middle of the Great Blizzard of 1888, with only a few days to spare. But she had not written either of her speeches. Susan took Elizabeth to her hotel room, gave her paper and a pencil, and locked the door. She could come out for meals and for an afternoon drive, Susan announced grimly, but otherwise Elizabeth was to stay there until the speeches were finished.

Elizabeth had often complained of Susan's demands. "One would think I was a machine," she once said, "that all I had to do was turn a crank and thoughts would bubble out like water." Fortunately, the crank did turn, and at the end of three days, Elizabeth emerged from her room, her work finished.

As it turned out, not only was she a success, but the meeting itself exceeded their expectations. Delegates from seven countries, representatives from fifty-three national women's organizations, and forty-four "pioneers" (thirty-six women, eight men) attended. And as a grand finale to the convention, President and Mrs. Cleveland invited everyone to a reception in the White House.

Lucy Stone did not attend the meeting, but some members of her organization were there. There was talk behind the scenes of uniting the two suffrage organizations. And then what? Elizabeth wondered. Would the conservatives take over? Even Susan, Elizabeth claimed, had become more conservative over the years, but not Elizabeth! She had become more radical, so of course she had mixed feelings when the merger actually went through two years later. In 1890 the two organizations were united into the new National American Woman Suffrage Association, and Elizabeth was nominated president. She did not decline. But she did leave for Europe right away.

This was her last trip to Europe. Her weight had become a problem, so she spent most of her hours, she said, "in the horizontal position . . . few in the perpendicular." When she had last tried to weigh herself, she had had to resort to a scale for weighing hay. She weighed 240 pounds, which was indeed heavy since she was only five feet three inches tall. She made no effort to reduce, so she must have known that she was still gaining weight and would find it increasingly difficult to get around. She was still able to work, however, and after eighteen months she returned home and took up where she had left off. She continued to write speeches for Susan, and even joined her in yet another campaign for suffrage in New York State. "What a set of jackasses we have at Albany this winter," she reported. "I have written several of them and they simply bray in return." And as usual the vote on suffrage was a resounding no.

Yet by 1890 women had made notable strides. They were able to vote in school elections in nineteen states, in city elections in Kansas, and in three states (Wyoming, Colorado, Oregon) they were granted full suffrage. Many colleges had opened their doors to women, and women had entered professions once closed to them. Elizabeth Blackwell, Lucy

Stone's sister-in-law, had become the first woman doctor. Married women could not only own property, but also they could make contracts, and under certain conditions they could get a divorce. And since the National American Woman Suffrage Association had more than 10,000 members, the future looked promising. Except for the churches. Elizabeth blamed preachers for holding women down. Right from the first, they had opposed woman suffrage. What would God say? What would St. Paul say? Elizabeth knew what St. Paul would say. He had a low opinion of women in Bible times and he was not the kind of man to change. In any case, Elizabeth decided to make the churches her next target. Susan objected. Why make more enemies? she asked. Stick to the vote!

Susan didn't like Elizabeth to stray from the subject of voting, but more and more this is what she did. She talked about religion; she talked about divorce, and again and again, Susan would fuss. Stick to the vote! she would say. Stick to the vote!

But Susan made headlines too. Once, listening to a minister preach a sermon in which he accused women of wanting freedom only for immoral purposes, Susan became so mad, she jumped to her feet. "You ought to be spanked!" she shouted at the minister right in the middle of the service. Cartoonists pictured Elizabeth and Susan as the "spanking team."

In her last major speech in 1892, Elizabeth took a philosophical point of view. Instead of bearing down on narrow issues, she reflected on the nature of life itself. She spoke from her heart as if she were sharing with her audience all that she had learned over the years. In the end, she said, everybody, men and women alike, were alone. They were responsible for themselves; no one could represent them. So it was not fair for men to shield women from participating fully in life. And it was demeaning for women to lean on men and not stand accountable for what they did or didn't do. Elizabeth called her speech "The Solitude of Self," and her followers agreed that it was the best speech of her career. All but Susan.

By this time Elizabeth had sold her house in Tenafly and had moved into the large city apartment where her bachelor son, Robert, lived. She would be eighty years old in 1895, and Susan asked her how she wanted to celebrate. Whatever ideas Elizabeth had, however, she never expected the lavish event that Susan (with Robert's help) dreamed up. The entire city took part. November 12 was declared in the New York papers as Stanton Day. Elizabeth herself, who over the years had been called everything from a "sexless old maid" to a "heretic," was suddenly hailed as the "Grand Old Woman of America." All day gifts arrived—everything from a grand piano to a hand-embroidered nightgown. And that evening the Grand Old Woman of America was taken to the Metropolitan Opera House, where 6,000 people were waiting to honor her.

The Opera House was decorated, top to bottom, with streamers and banners, while in the center of the stage stood a thronelike red plush chair, its sides and back covered with roses. A bank of white carnations stood at the back of the stage, with her name spelled out in red carnations. Seated on her throne, Elizabeth was entertained by music, speeches, and a historic tableau, "Then and Now." Of course she was called on to say something, and apparently Susan had made sure that she was prepared. Since she could not stand to deliver a speech, she had someone read it for her. It was a fine, generous speech. Susan approved of everything she said until she lit into the churches for being so backward. Susan must have groaned. Why couldn't Elizabeth have left the churches out of it? Why did she have to do battle on her birthday? The audience, however, did not seem ruffled. When they sang *Auld Lang Syne* at the end of the evening, they sang as if they meant it.

The next day Elizabeth seemed to be in a sentimental mood when she sat down to try out her new piano. She played and sang one old song after another, and when she had finished, she looked up at her nephew Robert, who had been listening. "Bob," she said suddenly, "life is a great mystery."

In spite of her handicaps, Elizabeth enjoyed her old age. She seemed to have outlived most of her anger, and her face, her children said, was radiant. She wrote her autobiography, which she dedicated to "Susan B. Anthony, my steadfast friend for half a century." And, of course, her steadfast friend continued to pester her for speeches. Elizabeth tried to persuade Susan to relax and take it easy, but she might as well have been talking to the wind. Next to Theodore Roosevelt, Susan B. Anthony was "the nearest thing to perpetual motion" that Elizabeth knew.

Elizabeth's health deteriorated until she was short of breath, almost totally blind, and hard of hearing. Her children didn't realize that she was so near the end, yet on October 26, 1902, they gathered at her side. Elizabeth seemed to know. She asked to be dressed. Then she asked to be helped to her feet.

75

Supporting herself by putting her hands on a table, she pulled herself straight, and for five or six minutes she stared ahead, as if she were facing an audience, as if she were making a silent speech. Or as if she were looking into the future. If so, she would have had to look eighteen years ahead to 1920 to see what she wanted to see. An amendment to the Constitution for woman suffrage. (Three other amendments had been squeezed in front of it, so this was the Nineteenth Amendment.)

Finally Elizabeth looked so tired, she was lowered into a chair and then back to bed. She fell asleep, and a few minutes later she was dead.

For Susan the whole world seemed silenced without Elizabeth Cady Stanton in it. There was "an awful hush," she said when she heard the news. "How lonesome I do feel!"

Elizabeth Cady Stanton
1815–1902

"EQUALITY FOR ALL"

"Men and angels, give me patience"

"...bear the consequences..."

"How long will the heathens rage?"

"...life is a great mystery."

# NOTES

*Page 1.* In summer they changed to blue dresses.

*Page 18.* Henry complained of the effect of the harsh Boston weather on his health, but if he thought Seneca Falls would be better, he was misinformed. He did know, however, that professionally he would be better off in New York than in Massachusetts.

*Page 25.* At first the women had planned that the men would be invited for the second day only, but when the men showed up on the first day, the women decided they could stay. There is disagreement among the sources about whether James Mott led the meetings on both days, or only on the second day.

*Page 38.* If her father did actually disinherit Elizabeth, he revised his will before he died.

*Page 42.* "all her friends"—Susan was referring primarily to members of Elizabeth's family.

*Page 46.* Before long Henry lost his job at the customs house due in great part to his son Daniel, who while working for him, took a bribe and forged his father's signature. At various times Henry worked for the *New York Herald Tribune*.

# Notes

*Page 61.* In 1876 the country celebrated the centennial anniversary of the Declaration of Independence, and of course women wanted a part in the festivities. Elizabeth Cady Stanton and Mathilda Jocelyn Gage wrote a new Declaration of Rights, and when the men refused to allow them to speak, a delegation marched up the platform, presented the chairman with a copy, and distributed the rest in the audience. Then they went outside and read it aloud to anyone who happened to be around.

*Page 66.* Harriot wrote one chapter in an effort to help her mother finish.

*Page 74.* Elizabeth read "The Solitude of Self" three times—once to the National American Woman Suffrage Association, and twice before different committees of Congress.

*Page 75.* In 1895 Elizabeth published *The Woman's Bible*. She had selected all the Biblical texts that mentioned women or that Elizabeth thought should have mentioned women, and added her own commentaries. Her purpose was to show how the church used such quotations to reduce women to a secondary place.

# BIBLIOGRAPHY

Bacon, Margaret Hope. *Mothers of American Feminism: The Story of Quaker Women in America* (New York: Harper & Row), 1986.

Banner, Lois W. *Elizabeth Cady Stanton: A Radical for Woman's Rights* (Boston: Little, Brown), 1980.

Barry, Kathleen. *Susan B. Anthony: A Biography of a Singular Feminist* (New York: New York University Press), 1988.

Bullard, Laura Curtis in *Our Famous Women,* ed. by Elizabeth Stuart Phelps. (Hartford: Hartford Publishing Co.), 1888.

Dubois, Ellen Carol, ed. *The Elizabeth Cady Stanton–Susan B. Anthony Reader* (Boston: Northeastern University Press), 1992.

Forster, Margaret. *Significant Sister: The Grassroots of Active Feminism, 1839–1939* (New York: Alfred A. Knopf), 1985.

Griffith, Elisabeth. *In Her Own Right: The Life of Elizabeth Cady Stanton* (New York: Oxford University Press), 1984.

Hare, Lloyd C. H. *The Greatest American Woman: Lucretia Mott* (New York: The American Historical Society), 1937.

Harper, Ida Husted. *The Life and Work of Susan B. Anthony,* 3 vols. (Indianapolis and Kansas City: Bowen-Merrill), 1899–1908.

Hays, Elinor Rice. *Morning Star: A Biography of Lucy Stone* (New York: Harcourt Brace), 1961.

Lutz, Alma. *Created Equal: A Biography of Elizabeth Cady Stanton.* (New York: John Day), 1940.

# Bibliography

*Report of the Woman's Rights Convention, Seneca Falls, N.Y., July 19–20, 1848* (Rochester: John Dick), 1848.

Scott, Ann Firor. *Making the Invisible Woman Visible* (Urbana and Chicago: University of Illinois Press), 1984.

Stanton, Elizabeth Cady. *Eighty Years and More: Reminiscences 1815–1897*. (Boston: Northeastern University Press), 1898–1993.

Stanton, Theodore, and Harriot Stanton Blatch, eds. *Elizabeth Cady Stanton as Revealed in Her Letters, Diary, and Reminiscences* (New York), 1922.

Venet, Wendy Hammand. *Neither Ballots nor Bullets: Women Abolitionists and the Civil War* (Charlottesville, VA: University Press of Virginia), 1991.

# INDEX

# Index

# Index

Emancipation Proclamation, 47
Embroidery, 2
Emma Willard's Female Seminary, 7
Europe, trips to, 67, 72

Fifteenth Amendment, 48, 54
Fourteenth Amendment, 48
  Susan B. Anthony and, 58–61
Fugitive Slave Law, 46

Gage, Mathilda Jocelyn, 65, 80n
Garrison, William Lloyd, 15, 33
Girls, proper behavior for, 2
Government, U.S., and woman's rights, 47, 48–49
Grant, Ulysses S., 61

Hunt, Jane, 20

International Council of Women, 68–72

Johnstown, New York, 1

Kansas, and woman's rights, 49–54

Lecture circuit, Elizabeth on, 56–58, 62–63
Lectures, by Elizabeth, 45–46. *See also* Speeches, by Elizabeth
Legislature, New York, 36–38
*Lily, The,* (temperance magazine), 28–29

Lincoln, Abraham, 45
  and slavery, 46, 47
London, World Anti-Slavery Convention, 10, 11
  and women, 12–15

Married women, legal status of, 2–5, 23–24, 73
Men, 20
  and "bloomers," 30
  Elizabeth and, 67
  laws made by, 5
  Susan's view of, 42
  and woman's rights, 48–49, 57–58
  and women, 23–24
Metropolitan Opera House, 74–75
Miller, Libby Smith, 29, 30, 62, 71
Ministers, and women. *See* Churches; Clergymen
Mott, James, 25, 55, 79n
Mott, Lucretia, 12, 15–16, 20, 43, 45, 55
  death of, 65
  and voting rights for women, 24
  at Seneca Falls Convention, 25
  and women's movement, 56

National American Woman Suffrage Association, 72, 73
National Woman's Rights Convention, Worcester, Massachusetts, 28
National Woman Suffrage Association, 56

# Index

# Index

# Index